the guide to owning a
Weimaraner

Anna Katherine Nicholas

The Publisher would like to thank the following owners of the dogs in this book: Amy Anderson, Doug Barber, Amanda Bedell, Sam Boggs, Judy Colan, Barbara Didjurgis, Jane Gamprecht, Ellen Grevatt, J. J. Gross, Cheryl Lent, Leonard and Judy Massey, Tracy Morgan, Dottie and John Morrill, Kimberly Petri, Carole Richards, Cindy Saxon, Cynthia Schneider, Audrey Soltis, C. E. Standley, Joyce Wirt.

T.F.H. Publications, Inc.
One TFH Plaza
Third and Union Avenues
Neptune City, NJ 07753

This book has been published with the intent to provide accurate and authoritative information in regard to the subject matter within. While every precaution has been taken in preparation of this book, the publisher and author assume no responsibility for errors or omissions. Neither is any liability assumed for damages resulting from the use of the information herein.

ISBN 0-7938-2211-4

Printed and bound in the United States of America

Printed and Distributed by T.F.H. Publications, Inc.
Neptune City, NJ

Contents

The Weimaraner breed is believed to have originated in Germany.

History of the Weimaraner

ORIGIN OF THE WEIMARANER

The forebears of these great dogs are the Red Schweisshunden, which trace their way back to the St. Hubert Hound. There is also the belief that some pointer stock was used to form the Weimaraner. The Red Schweisshunden accounts for the color indigenous to the breed; a genetic recessive in red or tan dogs can produce a silver-taupe color (sometimes even appearing almost lavender).

The Weimaraner was originally used as a pointer to flush out big game.

The Weimaraner's speed, agility, and courage helped him to develop into a premier hunting dog in Germany.

The breed, originally known as the Weimer Pointer, was used in big game hunting. The sponsor of these dogs was Grand Duke Karl August, head of the court at Weimer, who was born in the late 18th century. Weimer was the capital city of Thuringia, where several breeds had their beginning.

As civilization progressed, large game became scarce. However, birds and small game were still available and the Weimaraner, with his strength, tracking ability, speed, and courage, fit in well with this new type of hunting.

The Weimaraner Club of Germany was organized in Erfort on June 20, 1897. In order to own a Weimaraner, you had to belong to the club and agree to abide by and uphold all the rules of the club. In 1915, Major Robert aus der Herber shot over a Weimaraner for the first time. His devotion to the breed from that day on was complete, and, until his death in 1946, he was never without his favorite Weimaraners. Known as the "Father of the Breed," his contributions were many. He wrote many articles on the Weimaraner and also wrote a splendid book on the breed. He became president of the parent club in 1921.

Prince Hans von Ratibor introduced the Weimaraner to Austria in 1913. He felt that the Weimaraner was a new and better breed of all-around hunting dog. He became president of the newly formed Austrian Weimaraner Club.

In Germany, the breeding of all dogs was strictly controlled by a breeding warden who inspected all dogs to be used for such purposes. This is still true today.

HISTORY OF THE BREED IN AMERICA

Mr. Howard Knight of Providence, RI, an advertising executive and sportsman, was responsible for bringing the first Weimaraner to the United States. It was no easy task because the Germans didn't want to allow any of their dogs to come to America. Mr. Knight had to first join the Weimaraner Club of Germany and then agree to all of its rules. His first two purchases were brought to America in 1929, but alas, the dogs were both sterile. Knight continued to use these dogs in the field, however, and became even more determined to import other Weimaraners.

Finally, in 1938, he succeeded in bringing in five dogs: Mars a. d. Wulfsriede, Tasso a.d. Grutte, Aura v. Gaiberg, and two litter sisters, Adda and Dorle v. Schwarzen Kamp. Only Tasso was sterile. The other four formed the basis for Weimaraners in the United States.

World War II came along, precluding any further importation from Germany, with the exception of Suzanne v. Aspern. Mr. Knight's dogs had been the only ones that the Germans had legally permitted to be exported. In order to obtain them, he was compelled to protect the Weimaraner in every way, agreeing not to interbreed them with any other breed.

Mr. Knight eventually turned the responsibility for these dogs, plus three American-bred dogs produced by them, over to Mr. and Mrs. A. F. Horn of Hopkinson, MA, for showing, conditioning,

Through responsible breeding and the importation of dogs from Europe, the Weimaraner became a popular sporting dog in the US.

Ch. Colsidex Dauntless Applause, a top Weimaraner producer owned by Judy Colan.

and breeding. Mr. Knight wanted to share these dogs with others whose interests were similar to his own. This was a good choice as the Horns were also famous breeders of German Shepherd Dogs. It was questionable when there may be more Weimaraners imported, thus there would be no new bloodlines for some time. He didn't want his Weimaraners ruined by close linebreeding.

During the late 1940s, Mrs. Alva Deal imported several famous Weimaraners from the Harrasburg Kennels in Germany: Ch. Boddy of Harrasburg, Ch. Bert v. d. Harrasburg, Ch. Allie v. d. Murwitz, and Ch. Burt v. d. Harrasburg. The first Harrasburg dog was imported in 1947: Alto v. d. Harrasburg, who sired Ch. Count v. Houghton, who in turn sired the multiple Best in Show dog Ch. Val Knight Ranck. He was shown by both Anne Rogers Clark and Tom Crowe. Obviously, this was an important event as Ch. Val Knight Ranck produced 34 champion get in his lifetime.

The Weimaraner Club of America was founded in 1941, with the breed becoming officially recognized the following year. In 1943, the first Weimaraner was shown at Westminster.

The first two Weimaraners to complete their titles were Ch. Grafmar's Kreutz and Ch. Grafmar's Diana. There were very few Weimaraners shown, so it was difficult to finish a champion because there was not enough competition in the breed until the 1950s. Most Weimaraners hunted with their owners but did not appear in field trials until 1948. The first two to become dual champions were Palladian Perseus and Staubich v. Risen, RD, SDX. The first obedience title went to Aura v. Gaiberg, and his son, Ch. Grafmar Jupiter, who became the first UDT.

An important show dog, this is Ch. Colsidex Standing Ovation, the son of Ch. Colsidex Dauntless Applause and a multiple Best in Show winner. Owned by Judy Colan.

Ch. Burt v. d. Harrasburg took a Best in Show in Alaska and was the grandsire of the Best in Show winning Ch. Graves Rouge. Ch. Bert v. d. Harrasburg sired Best in Show winner Ch. Deal's Sporting True Aim II, who in turn sired Ch. Ann's Ricky Boy, CD, who was the first breeder/owner handled Weimaraner to go Best in Show.

Ricky was the grandsire of Ch. Shadowmar Barthaus Dorilio, also breeder/owner handled to Best in Show. Dorilio was the grandsire of Ch. Colsidex Dauntless Applause, who produced the five-time Best in Show winner Ch. Colsidex Standing Ovation. True Aim was also the grandsire of Best in Show winner Ch. von Gaiberg's Ord.

In 1962, Ch. Val Knight Ranck went First in the Sporting Group at Westminster. He also became the first multiple Best in Show Weimaraner, ending up with a total of nine wins. Ranck became the grandsire of Ch. Ronamax Rajah v. d. Reiteralm, also a multiple Best in Show dog. It is interesting to note that these two, Ovation and Rajah, plus Ch. Valmar Smokey City Ultra Easy who went back to Ch. Ann's Magic von der Reiteralm, were the three top sires in the breed: Ovation first, Ultra Easy second, and Rajah third.

It was in the 1970s that Weimaraners began to really do the winning that you see today. The top-winning Weimaraner of all time is the lovely bitch Ch. Aria's Allegra of Colsidex, sired by Ch. Colsidex Nani Follow That Dream out of Ch. Top Hats Spitfire. "Fergie" had a total of 27 Bests in Show. The top male Weimaraner is still Ch. Val Knight Ranck with his nine Bests in Show.

Weimaraner breeders and owners take great pride in the fact that the breed still retains its original hunting instincts.

Characteristics of the Weimaraner

Weimaraners make ideal family dogs. They are clean and well-mannered in the house and are a delight to have around. Good watch dogs, Weimaraners are quick to note danger. They love children and are content to play with them for hours.

Strongly bonded to their people, Weimaraners do not do well in kennel situations. They would consider separation from their human family to be the most horrible fate.

In appearance, the taupe color of the Weimaraner is probably his most distinguishing feature. Also, his eyes are an unusual color—light amber, gray, or blue-gray. The color has a tendency to change with excitement, sometimes almost appearing black.

The Weimaraner is a bird dog and one of the few pointing breeds to produce dual champions. The standard for the breed was written to describe a dog that could endure a day in the field. Weimaraners are great retrieving dogs; however, because of their lack of coat, they should not be expected to go into very cold water to retrieve.

IS THE WEIMARANER THE DOG FOR YOU?

You've decided that this is the breed for you. You want to own, train, show, and eventually breed Weimaraners. You have read everything that you can get your hands on about the breed, and you have a picture in your mind of the perfect dog. Before you bring a puppy home, there are a few more things you should do. Join a local Weimaraner club, as well as the national club. Get the *AKC Gazette* and any other magazines you can find and study them. See which breeders are winning consistently, regardless of who is showing the dogs. Go to the shows and carefully watch the

Puppies are adorable, but they are also a lot of hard work. If you do not have the time or inclination to train a puppy, an adult dog may be the best choice for you.

Because they bond strongly to their owners and enjoy being part of the family, Weimaraners are happiest as housedogs.

judging. Try to outguess the judge on which dog should win. Attend the National Specialty, if at all possible, talk to all of the exhibitors, and try to learn from them.

Learn which exhibitors produce Weimaraners that you feel are the correct type. Once you have narrowed your search down to three or four kennels, go visit them and see their brood bitches and the young stock that they have coming along. Find out what they currently have available or what they might have in the near future. Have patience and don't grab the first puppy that comes along.

Study structure and pedigrees. Once you have decided on a particular line, be willing to wait for the perfect puppy. Even if you have to wait a year, you can spend the time learning more about the breed and what you have to do to take special care of it. You may have to convince the breeder that you are really serious about getting into Weimaraners, because sometimes he may sell a fabulous puppy to someone that says they want to show and breed but then loose interest after they find that there is a certain amount of work involved.

Before going to look at puppies, you should have an idea of whether you want a male or a female. There are advantages to either one. Females tend to be homebodies, not wanting to roam. They also can be more affectionate, quieter, and easier to live with. If you are interested in breeding, obviously you will want a female.

Males, on the other hand, might want to roam if they get the opportunity. They also show breed character more strongly. If you are more interested in showing, a male might be more to your liking. If you will not be breeding or showing, you should plan on having your dog, male or female, neutered or spayed. It is much healthier for the dog and can help prevent cancer in many cases.

Do not be surprised if the breeder expects you to sign a sales contract. This is for your mutual benefit. The contract is a legal document that states the conditions of the sale. It will include the price of sale and the conditions that the breeder is guaranteeing, such as health concerns. The contract will also provide

Socialization is very important for your Weimaraner's well-being. Make sure the breeder of the puppy you choose has begun the socialization process.

Responsible breeders will breed only the best dogs to ensure the good temperament and health of the puppies. Four-week-old Weimaraner pups bred by Cheryl Lent.

for a refund of part of the sales price or replacement of the puppy if he turns out to have certain genetic diseases or other health problems.

It will state what you are agreeing to, such as if the dog is to be shown and/or bred. Sometimes a breeder will sell on a co-ownership, which allows him to keep partial control of a dog that he doesn't want to lose track of. Often a co-ownership will allow you to get a better dog than the average puppy for a lesser price. Be sure that you will be happy with this type of agreement, because if things don't work out later on, you might be very unhappy with what you are stuck with. Remember that the contract you sign is a legal document.

Before you make your final choice on a puppy, consider whether an older dog or older puppy would fit into your lifestyle better than a young puppy. If everyone in your household works a full day, your new pup would be alone too much of the time and you will have difficulty training him properly. If an older dog sounds interesting to you, you might get in touch with the Weimaraner

Dog ownership is a big responsibility, so research the Weimaraner's characteristics carefully before purchasing a puppy.

club; they have an active rescue committee that works to re-home Weimaraners that have been in unhappy situations and need new homes.

If you have decided that a puppy is what you want and you have found a breeder that you believe will work with you and your family, take the plunge and go to see the puppies. Let the breeder help you make your selection, as he knows his own line better than anyone. The entire litter should be well socialized and look healthy and happy. None of the puppies should be shy or standoffish, even with strangers.

Be sure you research your pup and his breeder as much as possible. Even with your breeder's help, the puppy that everyone feels will be a real winner might turn out to be an ugly duckling instead of a swan. In this case, if you have paid for a definite show puppy, the breeder will probably make an adjustment or will replace that puppy with another.

Take your Weimaraner puppy with you wherever you go. The more people he meets, the better socialized he will become.

The Standard for the Weimaraner

Each breed recognized and registered with the American Kennel Club has a standard that gives the reader a mental picture of what the specific breed should look like. All reputable breeders strive to produce animals that will meet the requirements of the standard. Also, many breeds were developed for a specific purpose, such as hunting, herding, working, guarding, etc. The sporting breeds, such as the Weimaraner, were all bred to hunt game of some type.

In addition to having dogs that look like proper Weimaraners, the standard ensures that the breed will have the personality, disposition, and intelligence that is as close as possible to an ideal specimen of the breed. If specific areas of the dog need a better description or more definition, breeders work together to create a revised standard. However, standards for any breed are never changed on a whim, and serious study and exchange between breeders takes place before any change is made.

OFFICIAL STANDARD FOR THE WEIMARANER

General Appearance—A medium-sized gray dog, with fine aristocratic features. He should present a picture of grace, speed, stamina, alertness and balance. Above all, the dog's conformation must indicate the ability to work with great speed and endurance in the field.

Height—Height at the withers: dogs, 25 to 27 inches; bitches, 23 to 25 inches. One inch over or under the specified height of each sex is allowable but should be penalized. Dogs measuring less than 24 inches or more than 28 inches and bitches measuring less than 22 inches or more than 26 inches shall be disqualified.

Head—Moderately long and aristocratic, with moderate stop and slight median line extending back over the forehead. Rather

The Weimaraner has an aristocratic appearance and presents an overall picture of strength and grace. Ch. Libertys Young American, owned by J. J. Gross and Cheryl Lent.

Ch. Zara's On Zee Rampage, owned by Carole Richards, has the refined head and clean-cut neck typical of the Weimaraner.

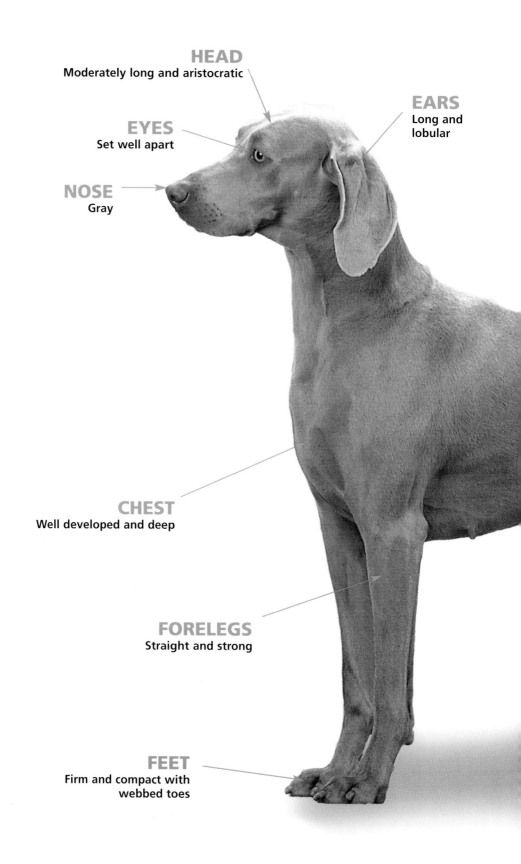

HEAD
Moderately long and aristocratic

EARS
Long and lobular

EYES
Set well apart

NOSE
Gray

CHEST
Well developed and deep

FORELEGS
Straight and strong

FEET
Firm and compact with webbed toes

BACK
Moderate in length, set in a straight line

TAIL
Docked

HINDQUARTERS
Well-angulated stifles and straight hocks

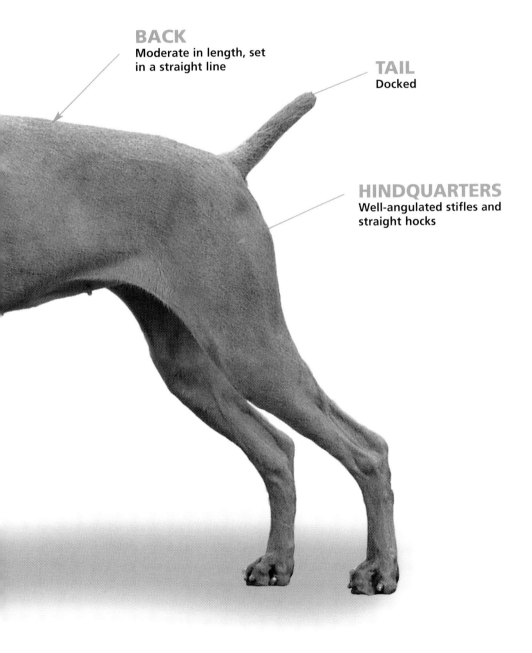

The Weimaraner's eyes should be light amber, gray, or blue-gray, and his expression should be kind, keen, and intelligent.

prominent occipital bone and trumpets well set back, beginning at the back of the eye sockets. Measurement from tip of nose to stop equals that from stop to occipital bone. The flews should be straight, delicate at the nostrils. Skin drawn tightly. Neck clean-cut and moderately long. Expression kind, keen and intelligent. *Ears*—Long and lobular, slightly folded and set high. The ear when drawn snugly alongside the jaw should end approximately 2 inches from the point of the nose. *Eyes*—In shades of light amber, gray or blue-gray, set well enough apart to indicate good disposition and intelligence. When dilated under excitement the eyes may appear almost black. *Teeth*—Well set, strong and even; well-developed and proportionate to jaw with correct scissors bite, the upper teeth

These two-day-old Weimaraner pups show off their unique stripes, which fade to a shade of gray by three or four days of age.

Overall, the Weimaraner should give the impression of power, balance, and athleticism.

protruding slightly over the lower teeth but not more than 1/16 of an inch. Complete dentition is greatly to be desired. **Nose**—Gray. **Lips and Gums**—Pinkish flesh shades.

Body—The back should be moderate in length, set in a straight line, strong, and should slope slightly from the withers. The chest should be well developed and deep with shoulders well laid back. Ribs well sprung and long. Abdomen firmly held; moderately tucked-up flank. The brisket should extend to the elbow.

Coat and Color—Short, smooth and sleek, solid color, in shades of mouse-gray to silver-gray, usually blending to lighter shades on the head and ears. A small white marking on the chest is permitted, but should be penalized on any other portion of the body. White spots resulting from injury should not be penalized. A distinctly blue or black coat is a disqualification.

Forelegs—Straight and strong, with the measurement from the elbow to the ground approximately equaling the distance from the elbow to the top of the withers.

Hindquarters—Well-angulated stifles and straight hocks. Musculation well developed.

Feet—Firm and compact, webbed, toes well arched, pads closed and thick, nails short and gray or amber in color. **Dewclaws**—Should be removed.

Tail—Docked. At maturity it should

measure approximately 6 inches with a tendency to be light rather than heavy and should be carried in a manner expressing confidence and sound temperament. A non-docked tail shall be penalized.

Gait—The gait should be effortless and should indicate smooth coordination. When seen from the rear, the hind feet should be parallel to the front feet. When viewed from the side, the topline should remain strong and level.

Temperament—The temperament should be friendly, fearless, alert and obedient.

FAULTS

Minor Faults—Tail too short or too long. Pink nose.

Major Faults—Doggy bitches. Bitchy dogs. Improper muscular conditions. Badly affected teeth. More than four teeth missing. Back too long or too short. Faulty coat. Neck too short, thick or throaty. Low-set tail. Elbows in or out. Feet east and west. Poor gait. Cowhocks. Faulty backs, either roached or sway. Badly overshot, or undershot bite. Snipy muzzle. Short ears.

Very Serious Faults—White, other than spot on the chest. Eyes other than gray, blue-gray or light amber. Black mottled mouth. Non-docked tail. Dogs exhibiting strong fear, shyness or extreme nervousness.

DISQUALIFICATIONS

Deviation in height of more than one inch from standard either way.

A distinctly long coat. A distinctly blue or black coat.

Approved December 14, 1971

Your Weimaraner's New Home

Before you actually pick up your new puppy, be sure you have the basic things you will need for his care. Most important is a crate. It is best to get one that will fit him as a grown dog, unless you get a very inexpensive one to start out with. Be sure to have safe, age-appropriate toys that he can play with, ones that he can't chew up and swallow. He will need a collar and leash that will

If you and your new puppy have a long ride home from the breeder's, plan to stop often and allow him plenty of time outside.

Prepare your home for your Weimaraner pup by providing him with plenty of safe toys to chew on.

You should plan on picking up your new puppy as early in the day as possible, thereby allowing him most of the day to become accustomed to his new home. Be sure to let the breeder know what time you plan on picking up the puppy so that he will know when and how much to feed him prior to the trip. If it is a long ride, both you and your puppy will probably want to take a break during the journey. Find a secluded spot to let him walk around for a few minutes. If he moves his bowels, praise him, and be sure that you pick up after him. You do not want to take him where there may have been other dogs because he could pick up an infection or worms.

BRINGING YOUR PUPPY HOME

When you arrive home, let the puppy investigate his new home. Remember that he will likely have an accident unless you watch him very carefully. If he appears to be looking for a place to go, whisk him outside or to a newspaper if that is how you are going to handle housetraining. After a short time, give him a light meal and a drink of water. Allow him to go potty again, then put him in his crate or exercise pen, where you have provided him with some type of bed. Do not overfeed him at this first meal, because he is likely to become sick. Also, do not allow him to drink too much water at one time.

Although all of your friends have heard about your new acquisition, hold off on allowing them to troop in to see him. Wait at least several days before

fit him now. You will have to get another one later on as he grows. Be sure to have plenty of newspaper on hand, because it will certainly come in handy when housetraining. You may also want to have a puppy-sized exercise pen that can be put in the kitchen or moved outdoors in nice weather.

Be sure to take your crate along when you bring your puppy home. Line it well with newspaper, so if he makes a mess in the crate or vomits, it will be absorbed and easier to keep clean.

Your Weimaraner puppy may be apprehensive about his new home, so be patient and let him explore his new surroundings.

Puppies are always playing—especially with their littermates. If your new puppy seems to miss his siblings or mother, be sure to pay extra attention to him.

introducing your puppy. Most likely his full vaccination series is not yet complete and it is safer that strange germs brought in on people's clothing be kept away.

THE FIRST NIGHT WITH YOUR WEIMARANER

The first few nights that your young Weimaraner spends away from his mother and his siblings are quite difficult for him. He will feel lonely, possibly cold, and will miss the heartbeat of his littermates when sleeping. To make him feel better, you can play a radio low to keep him company, or try putting a clock that has a loud tick in his bed with him. This will remind him of the heartbeat of his littermates and will soothe him. A cuddly toy might help in the first weeks, as well as a dim nightlight, as he is too young to be able to see in the dark. This will help in the event that he may want to leave his bed for a drink of water or to relieve himself.

If your Weimaraner pup whimpers during the night, there are two things you should not do. Do not rush to comfort him each time he cries, because he is smarter than you think and will soon realize how to get you to come running. The other thing not to do is to yell at him

THE GUIDE TO OWNING A WEIMARANER

or hit him. For this first night, you may want to give your puppy some extra attention, but do not keep this up or you will never be able to stop.

The pup will cry for awhile and then will settle down and fall asleep. Some puppies are worse than others, so you have to use your own judgement as to how far you allow it to go. Do not take your puppy to bed with you unless you plan on making this permanent; the puppy will feel that it is his right to be there if you allow it for several nights. If you have opted to have two puppies, it will make things considerably easier as they will have each other for company.

A happy and healthy Weimaraner pup is a reflection of his breeder's good care.

Caring for Your Weimaraner

YOUR WEIMARANER'S BEST FRIEND

One of the first things you should do after getting your Weimaraner puppy is to make an appointment with the veterinarian that you have decided to use. You should have checked him out ahead of time, asking friends that have pets who they use and who they have been happy

Whether a puppy or an adult, your Weimaraner will need regular checkups and good preventive care in order to live a long and healthy life.

Puppies receive their first immunities from nursing but soon need vaccinations to protect them from life-threatening diseases.

with. In most cases, the breeder that your puppy comes from will give you a record of the inoculations that the puppy has received and when he is due for his next vaccinations. The puppy should be checked over very thoroughly so that any medical problems will be found. Your breeder should have guaranteed against any genetic diseases, and you will know immediately if any show up. A stool sample should be taken along so that the puppy can be checked for worms.

Besides having your veterinarian check out your puppy, you should make it a point to go over the puppy yourself periodically, checking for things such as fleas, ticks, lumps, or even mats. If there is

Make sure your Weimaraner always has cool clean water to drink, especially when outside.

Choose a dog food that is nutritionally complete and adequate for your Weimaraner's stage of life. Puppies need a growth formula.

any problem, you will catch it early and can have your vet attend to it before it becomes more serious or life-threatening.

FEEDING YOUR WEIMARANER

Almost any dog food on the market will do well for your Weimaraner. It is not necessary to buy the most expensive brand by any means. It is usually better to pick one kind of dog food and stick to it. You can decide to use dry meal, either by itself or mixed with canned meat. The meal should be moistened. You can also use canned dog food, not pure meat. You can use what they call semi-moist, which comes in a plastic packet. This is especially good to use when traveling, as it does not require any refrigeration.

There are special diets recommended by your veterinarian, particularly for some health problems. The vet may also recommend a diet if you have let your Weimaraner get a little on the heavy side.

In general, supplements are not necessary, as most dog foods have everything in them that your Weimaraner needs, such as vitamins, minerals, etc. The only thing you might want to add is

Put your Weimaraner on a regular feeding schedule. Puppies will need to eat several small meals a day, while adults can be given one or two larger meals.

Because he was developed to work in the field, the Weimaraner's short coat requires very little grooming.

something for his coat to give gloss and shine. Be sure that your Weimaraner always has fresh cool water to drink. This is almost as important as his food.

Amount to Feed

Many factors will determine how much you feed your puppy. If he is well covered with flesh, shows good bone development and muscle, and is active and alert, then his diet is fine. A puppy will consume about twice the amount as would an adult of the same breed. When you pick up your puppy, ask your breeder to show you how much to feed the puppy at each meal, and that will be a good start for you. Your Weimaraner pup should eat his meal in about five minutes. Any leftover food should be discarded. If he never finishes his meal, you are probably giving him too much. If the puppy starts to look too fat or too thin, you should adjust the amount that he is getting. No two puppies or dogs will require the same amount of food.

When to Feed

It really doesn't matter what time of day you feed your puppy. You can pick a time that is convenient for you as long as he receives the needed amount of food. Puppies from 8 to 16 weeks of age need to be fed 3 to 4 times a day. Older puppies and young adults should be fed twice a day, and most adults do well on a once a day feeding. Whatever times you decide on, try to maintain a schedule because your dog will learn when to expect his food. If a dog that's normally enthusiastic about mealtime suddenly shows a lack of interest in food, you'll know something's not right.

GROOMING YOUR WEIMARANER

Very little needs to be done to keep your Weimaraner in tip-top shape. They do not have an undercoat, and thus hardly shed at all. Your Weimaraner generally will not need to be bathed unless he happens to get into something.

In terms of clipping, most people do not remove the whiskers because when Weimaraners are in the field, they enhance hunting ability.

The only two things that are necessary to do on a regular basis are trimming his nails and keeping your dog's teeth

The amount of food your dog requires will depend on his age and level of activity. Weimaraners that participate in field work will need extra energy.

cleaned. You can purchase a tooth scaler, which you can become quite adept at using.

Training Your Weimaraner

HOUSETRAINING

The first type of training you will want to undergo with your Weimaraner puppy is

Crate training is the easiest and fastest way to housetrain your Weimaraner.

housetraining. To achieve this, you can either use newspaper indoors or let your puppy go potty outside. Because your puppy will grow quite quickly, it is preferable to train him to go outside when weather permits.

For the first couple of weeks, he can be confined to his exercise pen in the house where you can use a layer of newspaper with torn up pieces on top. As long as the pup is kept worm-free, the feces should be rather easy to clean up.

Remember that a puppy cannot control his bowels or bladder until he is several months old, so watch him at prime times: after he wakes from a nap, after eating, and after playtime. He will usually start searching for a place to go and possibly start whimpering. You should quickly pick him up and place him on the newspaper or carry him outside. Hold him in position gently but firmly. He might act like he doesn't understand what you want, but if

Your Weimaraner pup will look to you, his owner, for the discipline he needs to become a well-mannered adult.

you keep putting him back where you want him to go, he will finally get the idea. When he does go, praise him lavishly to let him know how pleased you are with him.

The soiled newspaper must, of course, be immediately cleaned up and disposed of properly. Puppies do not like to use a dirty toilet anymore than you would. The puppy's potty area should be placed near the kitchen door, and as he gets older, it can be placed outside. From then on, it is easy to get the puppy to use it while he is outside. You will want him to relieve himself in a specific area of the yard—it is

better to train him in this way than to have him going in your flower beds or on the walkways. Generally, when a dog becomes dirty in his own home, it is because the owner was not consistent in housetraining when he was a puppy. Housetraining should never require any form of punishment because your dog relieving himself is a wholly natural act and, as with children, it requires your guidance and patience to be successful.

You will be given much advice on how to bring up your new Weimaraner puppy. Everyone you know will give you ideas on this subject: friends, neighbors, and even articles and books you may read on the subject and particular breed. Some of this advice will be sensible; some will be ridiculous. Keep an open mind and use your common sense. Let that prevail over ideas that may not be pertinent to your Weimaraner or your way of life.

BASIC TRAINING

Once your puppy has reached approximately three months of age, you can begin his basic training. Do not try to train him for more then 20 minutes at a time. At this young age, his attention span really can't go on for longer than that. You can, however, give him a lesson in the morning and at night. Always start and end the lesson on a positive note, and give him lots of praise; this will build his self-confidence.

Collar and Leash Training

Training a puppy to his collar and leash is quite easy. Place a soft nylon collar on him. Initially, he will try to bite at it or scratch or rub it off, but he will soon forget about it, especially if you play with him. Leave the collar on him for several hours at a time. Some people will leave the collar on at all times; others will only put the collar on when taking the dog out. If you plan on showing your Weimaraner, it is better not to leave the collar on because it will mark the fur. Even if you will not be showing him, purchase a narrow rolled collar to keep the fur from being marked.

Once the puppy has stopped paying attention to the collar, you can try attaching the leash to it. Let the puppy drag it along behind him for awhile. If he tries to chew it, pick it up and follow along with him, keeping it slack and going where he wants to go. You want him to get the feel of the leash. Repeat this several times a day and very soon your pup will become used to it.

Next, you should let the puppy realize that the leash can restrict his movements by pulling in on it. He will most likely pull, buck, or just sit down. Call the puppy to you, pulling lightly on the leash; give him lots of praise when he does come to you. Never drag the puppy or be too rough with him. It will take several days for the puppy to get the idea. Use praise to make your point.

The Sit Command

This is an easy exercise to teach your puppy; he should learn it in just a few lessons. Call the puppy to you and make a fuss over him. Place one hand on his hindquarters and the other under his upper chest. Say "Sit" in a pleasant voice (never harsh). At the same time, gently push down on the puppy's rear and push up under the chest. The puppy will be forced to sit. Lavish praise on the puppy.

PROFESSIONAL TRAINING

How do you go about this training? Well, it's a very simple procedure, pretty well standardized by now. First, if you can afford the extra expense, you may send your Weimaraner to a professional trainer, where in 30 to 60 days he will learn how to be a "good dog." If you enlist the

Your Weimaraner must learn to walk on a leash, not only for his safety, but also for the safety of others.

The sit command is an easy exercise to teach your Weimaraner. Once he learns to sit, you can move on to more difficult commands.

services of a good professional trainer, follow his advice about when to come to see the dog. No, he won't forget you, but too-frequent visits at the wrong time may slow down his training progress. And using a "pro" trainer means that you will have to go for some training, too, after the trainer feels your Weimaraner is ready to go home. You will have to learn how your Weimaraner works, just what to expect of him, and how to use what the dog has learned after he is home.

OBEDIENCE TRAINING CLASS

Another way to train your Weimaraner (many experienced Weimaraner people think this is the best) is to join an obedience training class right in your own community. There is such a group in nearly

every community nowadays. Here you will be working with a group of people who are also just starting out. You will actually be training your own dog, since all work is done under the direction of a head trainer who will make suggestions to you and also tell you when and how to correct your Weimaraner's errors. Then, too, working with such a group, your Weimaraner will learn to get along with other dogs. And, what is more important, he will learn to do exactly what he is told to do, no matter how much confusion there is around him or how great the temptation is to go his own way.

Write to your national kennel club for the location of a training club or class in your locality. Sign up. Go to it regularly—every

Once your Weimaraner has mastered basic obedience, he can participate in more advanced activities, such as agility or field tests.

This is Ch. Libertys Gone with the Wind, owned by Dr. John and Mrs. Jill Gross.

session! Go early and leave late! Both you and your Weimaraner will benefit tremendously.

TRAIN HIM BY THE BOOK

The third way of training your Weimaraner is by the book. Yes, you can do it this way and do a good job of it too. But in using the book method, select a book, buy it, study it carefully; then study it some more, until the procedures are almost second nature to you. Then start your training. But stay with the book and its advice and exercises. Don't start in and then make up a few rules of your own. If you don't follow the book, you'll get into jams you can't get out of by yourself. If after a few hours of short training sessions your Weimaraner is still not working as he should, get back to the book for a study session, because it's your fault, not the dog's! The procedures of dog training have been so well systemized that it must be your fault, since literally thousands of fine Weimaraners have been trained by the book.

After your Weimaraner is "letter perfect" under all conditions, then, if you wish, go on to advanced training and trick work.

Your Weimaraner will love his obedience training, and you'll burst with pride at the finished product! Your Weimaraner will enjoy life even more, and you'll enjoy your Weimaraner more. And remember—you owe good training to your Weimaraner.

Showing Your Weimaraner

If you are interested in eventually showing your Weimaraner, you should take him to show-handling classes. Go to dog shows to learn about what is involved in competition. Aside from enjoying dog shows, you will meet other people interested in Weimaraners and can talk to people from other breeds.

Besides obedience and conformation judging, you can participate in an event called agility. This is a dog sport that came to the US from England. The handler and dog work as a team, working through a timed obstacle course. The scoring is based upon the dog completing all of the obstacles, as well as the speed with which this is accomplished. Many dog shows include agility as part of the events, or there are shows that are strictly agility. A great deal of enthusiasm is generated by this sport, with loud encouragement from the handlers and the spectators.

Weimaraners make very wonderful tracking dogs. There are various degrees of tracking, starting with Tracking Degree,

If you are interested in showing your Weimaraner, you can learn about what is involved in competition by attending various dog shows.

TD; Tracking Dog Excellent, TDX; and Verible Service Tracking, VST.

You and your Weimaraner may also enjoy doing service work together in your community. Many people like to take their well-trained Weimaraners to nursing homes to visit the elderly. There are programs that offer certification to become a therapy dog.

YOUR WEIMARANER AND OBEDIENCE

If you are patient and enjoy working with your dog, study some of the excellent books available on the subject of obedience. Then consider teaching your canine friend these basic manners. If you need the stimulus of working with a group, find out where obedience training classes are held (usually your veterinarian, your dog's breeder, or a dog-owning friend can tell you).

If you are going to do it yourself, there are some basic rules that you should follow. You must remain calm and confident in attitude. Never lose your temper and frighten or punish your dog unjustly. Be quick, and lavish with praise each time a command is correctly followed. Make it fun for the dog and he will be eager to please you by responding correctly. Repetition is the keynote, but it should not be continued without recess to the point of tedium. Limit the training sessions to 10 or 15 minute periods at a time.

Formal obedience training can be followed, and very frequently is, by entering the dog in obedience competition to

Training your Weimaraner for competition can give both you and your dog a great sense of accomplishment and create a strong bond between you.

work toward an obedience degree or several of them, depending on the dog's aptitude and your own enjoyment. Obedience trials are held in conjunction with the majority of all-breed conformation dog shows, specialty shows, and frequently as separate specialty events. If you are working alone with your dog, a list of trial dates may be obtained from your veterinarian, your dog's breeder, or a dog-owning friend. The *AKC Gazette* lists shows and trials to be scheduled in the coming months, and if you are a member of a training class, you will find the information readily available.

The goals for which one works in the formal AKC Member or Licensed Trials are the following titles: Companion Dog (CD),

When you see the letters "CD" following a dog's name, you will know that this dog has satisfactorily completed the following exercises: heel on leash, heel free, stand for examination, recall, long sit, and long stay. CDX means that tests have been passed on all of those just mentioned plus heel free, drop on recall, retrieve over high jump, broad jump, long sit, and long down. UD indicates that the dog has additionally passed tests in scent discrimination (leather article), scent discrimination (metal article), signal exercises, directed retrieve, directed jumping, and group stand for examination. The letters "OTCh." are the abbreviation for the only obedience title that precedes rather than follows a dog's name. To gain an obedience trial championship, a dog that already holds a Utility Dog degree must win a total of 100 points and must win 3 firsts, under 3 different judges, in Utility and Open B Classes.

Because of their high degree of intelligence, eagerness to please, and athleticism, the Weimaraner is a natural for obedience work.

Companion Dog Excellent (CDX), and Utility Dog (UD). These degrees are earned by receiving three "legs," or qualifying scores, at each level of competition. The degrees must be earned in order, with one completed prior to starting work on the next. For example, a dog must have earned CD prior to starting work on CDX; then CDX must be completed before UD work begins. The ultimate title attainable in obedience work is Obedience Trial Champion (OTCh.).

There is also a Tracking Dog title (TD) that can be earned at tracking trials. In order to pass the tracking tests, the dog must follow the trail of a stranger along a path on which the trail was laid between 30 minutes and 2 hours previously. Along this track there must be more than two right-angle turns, at least two of which are well out in the open where no fences or other boundaries exist for the guidance of the dog or handler. The dog wears a harness and is connected to the handler by a lead 20 to 40 feet in length. Inconspicuously dropped at the end of the track is an article to be retrieved, usually a glove or wallet, which the dog is expected to locate and the handler to pick up. The letters "TDX" are the abbreviation for Tracking Dog Excellent, a more difficult version of the tracking dog test, with a longer track and more turns to be worked through.

THE WEIMARANER IN THE FIELD

The Weimaraner was developed to hunt and retrieve; it really is his heritage. The earlier dogs hunted with their masters in the field, but did not get involved in field trials until 1948. Ch. Bert v.d. Harrasburg was running in trials and was the first dog to win an Open All Age Stake in 1951, in competition with other sporting breeds. Working with a handler on foot, the breed was by nature a closer hunting dog and had to be encouraged to range as far as necessary for field trials. In the 1950s, Field Champion Fritz v. Wehman aus Rockledge, owned by Gilbert Wehman and handled by Chet Cummings, dominated in the field. He won the National Open in 1953, '56, '57, '58, and '60.

The first dual champion was Palladian Perseus and then Staubich v. Risen, SDC RD. It was quite awhile before Weimaraners had numerous dual champions, because it was hard to get enough dogs to compete. As the breed has become more popular, a good number of people are competing in field work and becoming interested in the field ability that is the heritage of the Weimaraner.

Am. Can. Ch. Zara's Winsome Zephyr, CGC JH NSD NRD V, owned by Carole Richards, is being trained to locate and point birds in the field.

This family of champion Weimaraners enjoys an autumn hunt with breeder and owner Carole Richards.

Field Ratings

There is a relatively new rating system called the AKC Pointing Breeds Hunting Test. Dogs must qualify four times for each level: Junior Hunter, Senior Hunter, or Master Hunter.

There are Shooting Dogs ratings:

NSD—Novice Shooting Dog. This determines whether young or untrained dogs have hunting aptitude. Guns are not fired in this test.

SD—Shooting Dog. This establishes that a dog has definite hunting ability.

SDX—Shooting Dog Excellent. This is the top award offered under the field ratings; dogs must be finished, fully broken bird dogs.

There are also retrieving ratings:

NRD—Novice Retrieving Dogs. The dog must retrieve a single bird within five minutes, either on land or water.

The Weimaraner excels in field trials because of his inherent retrieving instincts. Am. Can. Ch. Norman's Greywind Phoebe Snow, owned by Ellen Grevatt, proudly qualifies for her Junior Hunter title.

Ch. Ghostmar's Let's Talk Taffeta, JH CD SD NRD V, or "Kamali" owned by Jane Gamprecht, is being sent for the retrieve by Joleigh Sartiano.

In AKC hunting tests, Weimaraners can qualify for hunting titles, shooting dog ratings, and retrieving ratings. Kamali obtains her Novice Retrieving Dog rating by bringing back a water retrieve.

Successful showing requires dedication and preparation, but most of all, it should be enjoyable for both dog and handler. Ch. Greywind's High Flying Cloud, TD JH, owned by Ellen Grevatt, wins Best in Show.

RD—Retrieving Dog. This requires a much more involved retrieve.

RDX—Retrieving Dog Excellent. Again, this is a much more involved retrieve.

Another rating system for Weimaraners is the BROM (Bench Register of Merit). This was started in 1968 to recognize the top producing sires and dams. All records of wins are taken from the *AKC Gazette*. The system takes into consideration only the wins and accomplishments of the get, not of the sires and dams themselves. The BROM also gives credit to field and obedience wins of the get.

CONFORMATION SHOWS

When considering a Weimaraner for conformation, you should look for a puppy that happens to be born with a degree of physical perfection that closely approximates the standard by which the breed is judged in the show ring. Such a dog, when mature, should be able to win or approach his championship in good company at the larger shows. Upon finishing his championship, he is apt to be highly desirable as a breeding animal, and as a proven stud, will eventually command a high price for service.

Showing Weimaraners is a lot of fun—yes, but it is a highly competitive sport. While all the experts were once beginners, the odds are against a novice. You will be showing against experienced handlers, often people who have devoted a lifetime to breeding, picking the right ones, and then showing those dogs through to their championships. Moreover, the most perfect Weimaraner ever born has faults, and in your hands the faults will be far more evident than with the experienced handler who knows how to minimize those faults. These are but a few points on the sad side of the picture.

The experienced handler, as I say, was not born knowing the ropes. He learned—*and so can you!* You can if you will put in the same time, study and keen observation that he did. But it will take time!

KEY TO SUCCESS

First, search for a truly fine show prospect. Take the puppy home, raise him by the book, and as carefully as you know how, give him every chance to mature into the Weimaraner you hoped for. Work with him at home, even if you only spend 10 or 15 minutes a day with him. Regular training will eventually turn him into the show dog you desire. Train your Weimaraner to stack easily, to have his bite checked, and to move at the proper gait. Then start out at match shows, and

In conformation, your Weimaraner will be evaluated on how closely he conforms to the standard of the breed. These three champions enjoy the fruits of their labors.

Agility is just one of the many events that allows the Weimaraner to apply his natural talents to the competition ring.

once you both have a bit of experience and have built your confidence, go gunning for the big wins.

.Next step, read the standard by which the Weimaraner is judged. Study it until you know it by heart. Having done this, and while your puppy is at home growing into a normal, healthy Weimaraner, go to every dog show you can possibly reach. Sit at the ringside and watch Weimaraner judging. Keep your ears and eyes open. Do your own judging, holding each of those dogs against the standard, which you now know by heart.

In your evaluations, don't start looking for faults. Look for the virtues—the best qualities. How does a given Weimaraner shape up against the standard? Having looked for and noted the virtues, then note the faults and see what prevents a given Weimaraner from standing correctly or moving well. Weigh these faults against the virtues, since, ideally, every feature of the dog should contribute to the harmonious whole dog.

"RINGSIDE JUDGING"

It's a good practice to make notes on each Weimaraner, always holding the dog against the standard. In "ringside judging," forget your personal preference for this or that feature. What does the standard say about it? Watch carefully as the judge places the dogs in a given class. It is difficult from the ringside always to see why number one was placed over the second dog. Try to follow the judge's reasoning. Later try to talk with the judge after he is finished. Ask him questions as to why he placed certain Weimaraners and not others. Listen while the judge explains his placings, and, I'll say right here, any judge worthy of his license should be able to give reasons.

When you're not at the ringside, talk with

the fanciers and breeders who have Weimaraners. Don't be afraid to ask opinions or say that you don't know. You have a lot of listening to do, and it will help you a great deal and speed up your personal progress if you are a good listener.

THE NATIONAL CLUB

You will find it worthwhile to join the national Weimaraner club and to subscribe to its magazine. From the national club, you will learn the location of an approved regional club near you. Now, when your young Weimaraner is six to ten months old, find out the dates of match shows in your section of the country. These differ from regular shows only in that no championship points are given. These shows are especially designed to launch young dogs (and new handlers) on a show career.

ENTER MATCH SHOWS

With the ring deportment you have watched at big shows firmly in mind and practice, enter your Weimaraner in as many match shows as you can. When in the ring, you have two jobs. One is to see to it that your Weimaraner is always being seen to his best advantage. The other job is to keep your eye on the judge to see what he may want you to do next. Watch only the judge and your Weimaraner. Be quick and be alert; do exactly as the judge directs. Don't speak to him except to answer his questions. If he does something you don't like, don't say so. And don't irritate the judge (and everybody else) by constantly talking and fussing with your dog.

In moving about the ring, remember to keep clear of dogs beside you or in front of you. It is my advice to you *not* to show your Weimaraner in a regular point show until he is at least close to maturity and after both you and your dog have had time to perfect ring manners and poise in the match shows.

The attention and training you give to your Weimaraner when preparing for conformation can only benefit your relationship with your dog.

Your Healthy Weimaraner

PUPPY HEALTH

Vaccinations

Every Weimaraner puppy should be vaccinated against the major canine diseases. These are distemper, leptospirosis, hepatitis, and canine parvovirus. Your puppy may have received a temporary vaccination against distemper before you

Your veterinarian should put your Weimaraner on a vaccination schedule as a puppy and continue with regular booster shots throughout his life.

Your Weimaraner pup will have a good start in life if his mother is healthy and well adjusted.

purchased him, but be sure to ask the breeder to be certain.

The age at which vaccinations are given can vary, but will usually be when the pup is 8 to 12 weeks old. By this time, any protection given to the pup by antibodies received from his mother via her initial milk feeds will be losing their strength.

The puppy's immune system works on the basis that the white blood cells engulf and render harmless attacking bacteria. However, they must first recognize a potential enemy.

Vaccines are either dead bacteria or they are live, but in very small doses. Either type prompts the pup's defense system to attack them. When a large attack then comes (if it does), the immune system recognizes it and massive numbers of lymphocytes (white blood corpuscles)

are mobilized to counter the attack. However, the ability of the cells to recognize these dangerous viruses can diminish over a period of time. It is therefore useful to provide annual reminders about the nature of the enemy. This is done by means of booster injections that keep the immune system on its alert. Immunization is not 100-percent successful, but is very close. Certainly it is better than giving the puppy no protection.

Dogs are subject to other viral attacks, and if these are of a high-risk factor in your area, your vet will suggest you have the puppy vaccinated against these as well.

Your puppy or dog should also be vaccinated against the deadly rabies virus. In fact, in many places it is illegal for your

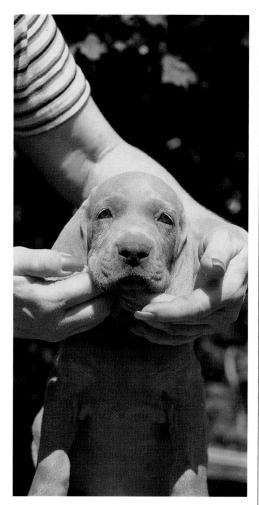

Regular physical exams will help you keep on top of any problems your Weimaraner may experience.

problems than are carelessly bred and neglected animals. Your knowledge of how to avoid problems is far more valuable than all of the books and advice on how to cure them. Respectively, the only person you should listen to about treatment is your vet. Veterinarians don't have all the answers, but at least they are trained to analyze and treat illnesses and are aware of the full implications of treatments, which most others are not. This does not mean a few old remedies aren't good standbys when all else fails, but in most cases modern science provides the best treatments for disease.

PHYSICAL EXAMS

Your puppy should receive regular physical examinations or checkups. These come in two forms. One is obviously

All dogs deserve good health care—your Weimaraner will thank you for it.

dog not to be vaccinated. This is to protect your dog, your family, and the rest of the animal population from this deadly virus that infects the nervous system and causes dementia and death.

Dogs, like all other animals, are capable of contracting problems and diseases that, if listed, would seem overwhelming. However, in most cases these are easily avoided by sound husbandry—meaning well-bred and well-cared-for animals are less prone to developing diseases and performed by your vet, and the other is a day-to-day procedure that should be done by you. Apart from the fact the exam will highlight any problem at an early stage, it is an excellent way of socializing the pup to being handled.

To do the physical exam yourself, start at the head and work your way around the body. You are looking for any sign of lesions or any indication of parasites on the pup. The most common parasites are fleas and ticks.

FIGHTING FLEAS

Fleas are very mobile and may be red, black, or brown in color. The adults suck the blood of the host, while the larvae feed on the feces of the adults, which is rich in blood. Flea "dirt" may be seen on the pup as very tiny clusters of blackish specks that look like freshly ground pepper. The eggs of fleas may be laid on the puppy, though they are more commonly laid off the host in a favorable place, such as the bedding. They normally hatch in 4 to 21 days, depending on the temperature, but they can survive for up to 18 months if temperature conditions are not favorable. The larvae are maggot-like and molt a couple of times before forming pupae, which can survive long periods until the temperature or the vibration of a nearby host causes them to emerge and jump on a host.

Weimaraners that spend a lot of time in the field should be carefully examined for parasites like fleas and ticks before coming inside.

There are a number of effective treatments available, and you should discuss them with your veterinarian, then follow all instructions for the one you choose. Any treatment will involve a product for your puppy or dog and one for the environment and will require diligence on your part to treat all areas and thoroughly clean your home and yard until the infestation is eradicated.

THE TROUBLE WITH TICKS

Ticks are arthropods of the spider family, which means they have eight legs (though the larvae have six). They bury their headparts into the host and gorge on its blood. They are easily seen as small grain-like creatures sticking out from the skin. They are often picked up when dogs play in fields, but may also arrive in your yard via wild animals—even birds—or stray cats and dogs. Some ticks are species-specific, others are more adaptable and will host on many species.

The most troublesome type of tick is the deer tick, which spreads the deadly Lyme disease that can cripple a dog (or a person). Deer ticks are tiny and very hard to detect. Often, by the time they're big enough to notice, they've been feeding on the dog for a few days—long enough to do their damage. Lyme disease was named for the area of the United States in which it was first detected—Lyme, Connecticut—but has now been diagnosed in almost all parts of the US. Your veterinarian can advise you of the danger to your dog(s) in your area, and may suggest your dog be vaccinated for Lyme. Always go over your dog with a fine-toothed flea comb when you come in from walking through any area that may harbor deer ticks, and if your dog is acting unusually sluggish or sore, seek veterinary advice.

Weimaraners love to do what they do best—retrieve. However, for the safety of your dog, make sure he is properly trained and conditioned before allowing him to participate in dog sports.

Dogs can pick up parasites or diseases from other dogs, so be sure that your Weimaraner has all his vaccinations before taking him out to socialize.

Attempts to pull a tick free will invariably leave the headpart in the pup, where it will die and cause an infected wound or abscess. The best way to remove ticks is to dab a strong saline solution on them, or you can use iodine or alcohol. This will numb them, causing them to loosen their hold, at which time they can be removed with forceps. The wound can then be cleaned and covered with an antiseptic ointment. If ticks are common in your area, consult with your vet for a suitable pesticide to be used in kennels, on bedding, and on the puppy or dog.

INSECTS AND OTHER OUTDOOR DANGERS

There are many biting insects, such as mosquitoes, that can cause discomfort to a puppy. Many diseases are transmitted by the males of these species.

A pup can easily get a grass seed or thorn lodged between his pads or in the folds of his ears. These may go unnoticed until an abscess forms. This is where your daily check of your Weimaraner will do a world of good. If your puppy has been playing in long grass or places where there may be thorns, pine needles, wild animals, or parasites, the checkup is a wise precaution.

SKIN DISORDERS

Apart from problems associated with lesions created by biting pests, a puppy may fall foul to a number of other skin disorders; for example, ringworm, mange, and eczema. Ringworm is not caused by a worm but a fungal infection. It manifests itself as a sore-looking bald circle. If your puppy should have any form of bald patches on him, let your veterinarian check him over; a microscopic examination can confirm the condition. Many old remedies for ringworm exist, such as iodine, carbolic acid, formalin, and other tinctures, but modern drugs are superior.

Fungal infections can be very difficult to treat and even more difficult to eradicate because of the spores. These can withstand most treatments, other than burning, which is the best thing to do with bedding once the condition has been confirmed.

Mange is a general term that can be applied to many skin conditions where the hair falls out and a flaky crust develops and falls away. Often, dogs will scratch themselves, and this invariably is worse than the original condition, for it opens lesions that are then subject to viral, fungal, or parasitic attack. The cause of the problem can be various species of mites. These either live on skin debris and the hair follicles, which they destroy, or they bury themselves just beneath the skin and feed on the tissue. Applying general remedies from pet stores is not recommended because it is essential to identify the type of mange before a specific treatment can be effective.

Eczema is another nonspecific term applied to many skin disorders. The condition can be brought about in many ways. Sunburn, chemicals, allergies to foods, drugs, pollens—even stress—can all produce a deterioration of the skin and coat. Given the range of causal factors, treatment can be difficult because the problem is one of identification. It is a case of taking each possibility at a time and trying to correctly diagnose the matter. If the cause is of a dietary nature, then you must remove one item at a time in order to find out if the dog is allergic to a given food. It could, of course, be the lack of a nutrient that is the problem, so if the condition persists, you should consult your veterinarian.

INTERNAL DISORDERS

It cannot be overstressed that it is very foolish to attempt to diagnose an internal disorder without the advice of a veterinarian. Take a relatively common problem such as diarrhea. It might be caused by nothing more serious than the puppy hogging a lot of food or eating something that he has never previously eaten. Conversely, it could be the first indication of a potentially fatal disease. It's up to your veterinarian to make the correct diagnosis.

The following symptoms, especially if they accompany each other or are progressively added to earlier symptoms, mean you should visit the veterinarian right away:

Continual vomiting: All dogs vomit from time to time, and this is not necessarily a sign of illness. They will eat grass to induce vomiting. It is a natural cleansing process common to many carnivores. However, continued vomiting

The good care your give your Weimaraner will be evident in his healthy appearance and overall well-being.

is a clear sign of a problem. It may be a blockage in the pup's intestinal tract, it may be induced by worms, or it could be due to any number of diseases.

Diarrhea: This, too, may be nothing more than a temporary condition due to many factors. Even a change of home can induce diarrhea, because this often stresses the pup, and invariably there is some change in the diet. If it persists more than 48 hours, something is amiss. If blood is seen in the feces, waste no time at all in taking the dog to the vet.

Running eyes and/or nose: A pup might have a chill and this will cause the eyes and noise to weep. Again, this should quickly clear up if the puppy is placed in a warm environment and away from any drafts. If it does not, and especially if a mucous discharge is seen, then the pup has an illness that must be diagnosed.

Coughing: Prolonged coughing is a sign of a problem, usually of a respiratory nature.

Wheezing: If the pup has difficulty breathing and makes a wheezing sound when breathing, then something is wrong.

Crying: This might only be a minor problem due to the hard state of the feces, but it could be more serious, especially if the pup cries when urinating. Obviously, if you do not handle a puppy

Puppies are usually filled with endless energy, so if your Weimaraner pup seems unusually listless, consult your veterinarian.

with care he might yelp. However, if he cries even when lifted gently, then he has an internal problem that becomes apparent when pressure is applied to a given area of the body. Clearly, this must be diagnosed.

Refuses food: Generally, puppies and dogs are greedy creatures when it comes to feeding time. Some might be fussier than others, but none should refuse more than one meal. If they go for a number of hours without showing any interest in their food, then something is not as it should be.

General listlessness: All puppies have their off days when they do not seem their usual cheeky, mischievous selves. If this condition persists for more than two days, then there is little doubt of a problem. They may not show any of the signs listed, other than perhaps a reduced interest in their food. There are many diseases that can develop internally without displaying obvious clinical signs. Blood, fecal, and other tests are needed in order to identify the disorder before it reaches an advanced state that may not be treatable.

WORMS

There are many species of worms, and a number of these live in the tissues of dogs and most other animals. Many create no problem at all, so you are not even aware they exist. Others can be tolerated in small levels, but become a major problem if they number more than a few. The most common types seen in dogs are roundworms and tapeworms. While roundworms are the greater problem, tapeworms require an intermediate host so are more easily eradicated.

Roundworms of the species toxocara canis infest the dog. They may grow to a length of 8 inches (20 cm) and look like strings of spaghetti. The worms feed on the digesting food in the pup's intestines.

In chronic cases the puppy will become pot-bellied, have diarrhea, and will vomit. Eventually, he will stop eating, having passed through the stage when he always seems hungry. The worms lay eggs in the puppy and the eggs pass out in his feces. They are then either ingested by the pup, or they are eaten by mice, rats, or beetles. These may then be eaten by the puppy and the life cycle is complete.

Larval worms can migrate to the womb of a pregnant bitch or to her mammary glands, and this is how they pass to the puppy. The pregnant bitch can be wormed, which will help. The pups can and should be wormed when they are about two weeks old. Repeat worming every 10 to 14 days and the parasites

If your Weimaraner becomes ill or sustains an injury, whether at home or in the field, acting quickly and appropriately can help save his life.

Proper eating habits and a consistent diet will help your Weimaraner avoid certain gastric problems such as bloat.

should be removed. Worms can be extremely dangerous to young puppies, so you should be sure the pup is wormed as a matter of routine.

Tapeworms can be seen as tiny rice-like eggs sticking to the puppy's or dog's anus. They are less destructive, but still undesirable. The eggs are eaten by mice, fleas, rabbits, and other animals that serve as intermediate hosts. They develop into a larval stage and the host must be eaten by the dog in order to complete the chain. Your vet will supply a suitable remedy if tapeworms are seen or suspected. The vet can also do an egg count on the pup's feces under the microscope; this will indicate the extent of an infestation.

There are other worms, such as hookworms and whipworms, that are also blood suckers. They will make a pup anemic, and blood might be seen in the feces, which can be examined by the vet to confirm their presence. Cleanliness in all matters is the best preventative measure for all worms.

BLOAT (GASTRIC DILATATION)

This condition has proved fatal in many dogs, especially large and deep-chested breeds. However, any dog can get bloat. It is caused by gases building up in the stomach, especially in the small intestine. What happens is that carbohydrates are fermented and release gases. Normally, these gases are released by belching or by being passed from the anus. If for any reason these exits become blocked (such as if the stomach twists due to physical exertion), the gases cannot escape and the stomach simply swells and places pressure on other organs, sometimes cutting off the blood supply to the heart or causing suffocation. Death can easily follow if the condition goes undetected.

The best preventative measure is not to feed large meals or exercise your puppy or dog immediately after he has eaten. You can reduce the risk of flatulence by feeding more fiber in the diet, not feeding too many dry biscuits, and possibly by adding activated charcoal tablets to the diet.

ACCIDENTS

All puppies will get their share of bumps and bruises due to the rather energetic way they play. These will usually rectify themselves over a few days. Small cuts should be bathed with a suitable disinfectant and then smeared with an antiseptic ointment. If a cut looks more serious, then stem the flow of blood with a towel or makeshift tourniquet and rush the pup to the veterinarian. Never apply so much pressure to the wound that it might restrict the flow of blood to the limb.

In the case of burns you should apply cold water or an ice pack to the surface. If the burn was due to a chemical, then this must be washed away with copious

The athletic Weimaraner loves to be active, and as long as your dog is in good condition, he will be able to perform with ease.

The pup may go into shock, depending on the severity of the burn, and this will result in a lowered blood pressure, which is dangerous and the reason the pup must receive immediate veterinary attention.

If a broken limb is suspected, try to keep the animal as still as possible. Wrap your pup or dog in a blanket to restrict movement and get him to the veterinarian as soon as possible. Do not move the dog's head so it is tilting backward, as this might result in blood entering the lungs.

Do not let your pup jump up and down from heights, as this can cause considerable shock to the joints. Like all youngsters, puppies do not know when enough is enough, so you must do all their thinking for them.

Provided you apply strict hygiene to all aspects of your puppy's husbandry, and you make daily checks on his physical state, you have done as much as you can to safeguard him during his most vulnerable period. Routine visits to your veterinarian are also recommended, especially while the puppy is under one year of age.

Curious Weimaraners can get in all sorts of trouble if they are not carefully supervised. Make sure you keep a close eye on your dog at all times, especially when outside.

amounts of water. Apply an antibiotic ointment to the burn while it is healing if necessary. Trim away the hair if need be. If the burns appear to be severe, wrap the dog in a blanket and rush him to the vet.

Index

Photo Credits